GO FACTS SPACE

Our Future in Space

A & C BLACK • LONDON

Our Future in Space

contents

© Blake Publishing 2006
Additional material © A & C Black Publishers Ltd 2006

First published in Australia in 2006 by Blake Education Pty Ltd

This edition published in the United Kingdom in 2006 by
A & C Black Publishers Ltd, 38 Soho Square, London W1D 3HB
www.acblack.com

Hardback edition
ISBN-10: 0-7136-8387-2
ISBN-13: 978-0-7136-8387-5

Paperback edition
ISBN-10: 0-7136-8385-6
ISBN-13: 978-0-7136-8385-1

A CIP record for this book is available from the British Library.

Written by Maureen O'Keefe
Publisher: Katy Pike
Editor: Paul O'Beirne
Design and layout by The Modern Art Production Group

Photo credits: p7 (tl), p12 (tl, br), p13 (top, bl), p23 (br), p26 (tr), p29 (bl) pictures
courtesy NASA; p7 (tr), p17 (top), p21 (top), p25 (tr) (australian picture library);
p17 (br), p27 (br) (aap). Illustration on p25: Luke Jurevicius and Toby Quarmby.

Printed in China by WKT Company Ltd.

This book is produced using paper that is made from wood grown in managed,
sustainable forests. It is natural, renewable and recyclable. The logging and
manufacturing processes conform to the environmental regulations of the country
of origin.

What People Need to Survive

To survive, humans need water to drink, air to breathe, food to eat and reasonable temperatures. None of these are available on the other planets in our solar system.

Water is essential for human survival. Liquid water has not yet been discovered on the other planets in our solar system. Before we can travel deeper into space, we need to ensure a reliable supply of fresh water for space travellers.

In space, we need to recreate an atmosphere similar to Earth's. Our atmosphere contains oxygen, which humans need to breathe for survival. The carbon dioxide that we breathe out is taken in by plants. Plants recycle the carbon dioxide and produce oxygen, which goes back into the atmosphere.

Presently, we take our food with us when we venture into space. However, if we intend to go deeper into space, we must be able to replenish our food supply without relying on Earth.

The Sun's energy provides us with light and heat. This energy is already being used by the International Space Station for all its energy needs. However, once we move towards Mars in our exploration, we may be unable to use the Sun's energy. This is because the further we travel from the Sun, the less power we can generate from it.

There are places on Earth where not all the requirements for human survival are met. Deserts lack water, oceans lack air and shelter, and very cold places lack food and warmth. It is possible that we can learn how to live in space by experimenting with living in some of these inhospitable places here on Earth.

GO FACT!

DID YOU KNOW?

Oxygen is the most important of human needs. Humans can live for days without food or water, but only minutes without oxygen. Earth is the only known place that has a breathable atmosphere. The Moon has no atmosphere, and the Martian atmosphere is 95% carbon dioxide.

Liquid water is essential for life to evolve and survive. For this to happen, chemical reactions must take place so that simple chemicals can combine to form more complex ones. Chemical reactions occur in liquid water.

5

Space Stations

Space stations have orbited Earth for more than 35 years. The earliest attempts at living in space occurred on the Salyut, Skylab and Mir space stations.

Salyut

Space stations have orbited Earth since 1971. In that year, the first space station, Salyut 1, was launched by the former **Soviet Union**. Between 1971 and 1982 there were seven Salyut stations. **Cosmonauts** travelled to these stations by spacecraft. During this time, unmanned supply ships were developed to **dock** with the Salyut station.

Skylab

In 1973, the United States launched its first space station which was called Skylab. It remained in orbit until 1979. Onboard Skylab, astronauts conducted experiments on the effects of living in space on the human body, and took X-rays of the Sun.

Mir

In 1986, the Soviet Union launched a new space station called Mir. It remained in orbit until 2001. Both manned and unmanned spacecraft docked with Mir, transporting crews and cargo to and from the station. In 1995, the Atlantis space shuttle docked with Mir, and the American crew from Atlantis went aboard.

While on Mir, scientists did experiments to determine how people, animals and plants can survive in space, how we can build technology in space and how to build future space stations.

More than 100 astronauts and cosmonauts lived on Mir during its time in space – but not at the same time!

Mir's mission was ended by scientists in 2001. A cargo ship docked with Mir, slowed its orbit and pushed it into Earth's upper atmosphere. Much of the station disintegrated in the atmosphere. The remaining pieces became a meteor shower which fell into the South Pacific Ocean.

Space stations are either launched in one piece, or in separate pieces, and assembled in space. Skylab was launched in one piece and then manned by a crew later, whereas Mir was launched piece by piece and put together in space by cosmonauts.

GO FACT!

DID YOU KNOW?
Many of the experiments conducted on Skylab investigated how astronauts adapted to extended periods of **microgravity**.

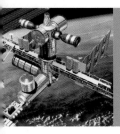

Astronauts began living on the International Space Station (ISS) in 2000 even though it wasn't completely finished.

Construction

The ISS is being assembled in space. The experience gained from constructing previous space stations is being used to build the new ISS in orbit. It will require 45 assembly missions in total, using space shuttles and other launch vehicles. Astronauts and cosmonauts on these spacecraft will build and maintain the station, doing over 1000 spacewalk hours.

Research

There will be six laboratories on the completed station. These will be used for research into microgravity and how it affects animals and plants. This research will look at how humans lose bone **density** and muscle strength while in space. The station will provide a place to learn how we can live somewhere other than Earth.

Scientists will also research new ways of constructing equipment in space, and test new technologies, such as satellites and **solar cells**. Medical research in space is very accurate. Microgravity means that experiments are conducted in a pure environment – the very small amount of gravity doesn't distort the results.

The first ISS crew was launched from Russia in October 2000.

A working life-support system needs to be established on the ISS if people are going to undertake **interplanetary** space voyages, such as visiting Mars.

The ISS will be used for experiments in physics, biology, fire fighting, medicine and climate.

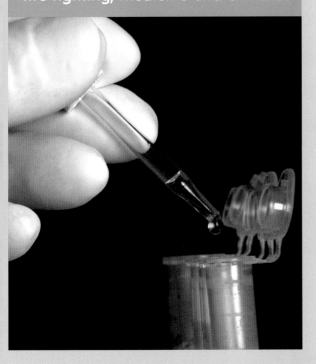

GO FACT!

DID YOU KNOW?

When completed, the International Space Station will be four times larger than Mir.

Power for the ISS

The Sun provides energy for people on the International Space Station, just like it does for us on Earth.

How is the ISS powered?

All the systems on board the ISS need electrical power. Electricity operates the air systems that allow the astronauts to breathe, controls the temperature and runs the water and food systems. Our Sun provides power for the space station.

Power is generated and supplied to the station by eight large, wing-shaped structures, called **solar arrays**. These are panels of solar cells, which convert sunlight to electricity.

The ISS takes about 95 minutes to orbit Earth. It is in sunlight for two-thirds of its orbit. During this time, half the power generated by the solar arrays is used to power the laboratories and other rooms on the space station, and all the life-support systems. The other half of the power charges the three nickel-hydrogen batteries on board the station.

For about one-third of its orbit, the ISS passes through Earth's shadow and is in darkness. During this time the station relies on the nickel-hydrogen batteries to supply its power needs.

10

When working to full capacity, the ISS will have about 100 computers, all requiring power.

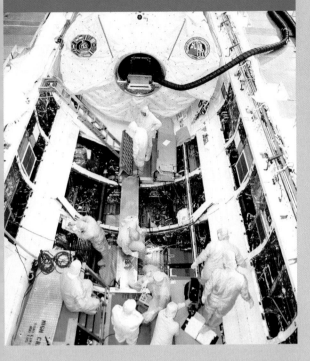

Since the ISS was established, there have been over 320 hours of spacewalks.

The ISS has robotic arms to help astronauts on spacewalks. They work like 'cherry pickers' and move astronauts to work areas. The arms are also used to move large pieces of equipment needed by astronauts.

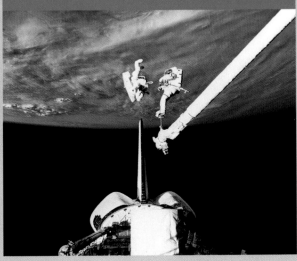

GO FACT!

DID YOU KNOW?

The ISS will never return to Earth, so any repairs must be done in orbit.

Living on a Space Station

There is very little gravity in orbit, so it is known as microgravity. This means things are done differently from the way they are done on Earth.

Eating and drinking

Food is mainly **dehydrated** or **heat-stabilised**. Drinks are also dehydrated. Once food has been rehydrated and heated, astronauts eat the food on magnetic trays. The food has some moisture, so it sticks to the spoon. The magnetic tray means that the knives, forks and spoons stick to the trays and don't float away. A straw is used for drinks.

Sleeping

Astronauts sleep in sleeping bags attached to the walls of the station. They zip themselves in so they don't float out of the bag while asleep. It is very important that astronauts sleep near a ventilator fan which keeps air moving. This is because warm air doesn't rise in space, so without a fan, the astronauts would be surrounded by the carbon dioxide that they have exhaled and not get enough oxygen.

Exercising

The ISS has treadmills and exercise bikes. Lower back and leg muscles aren't used much in space so astronauts need to do two hours of exercise a day to stop muscles losing tone and mass. Astronauts need to be strapped onto the equipment so they don't float away.

In space, a small amount of force moves you a long way. To move from the floor to the ceiling, all you need to do is rise up on your toes. Astronauts move around by 'flying', after learning how to slow down and avoid objects.

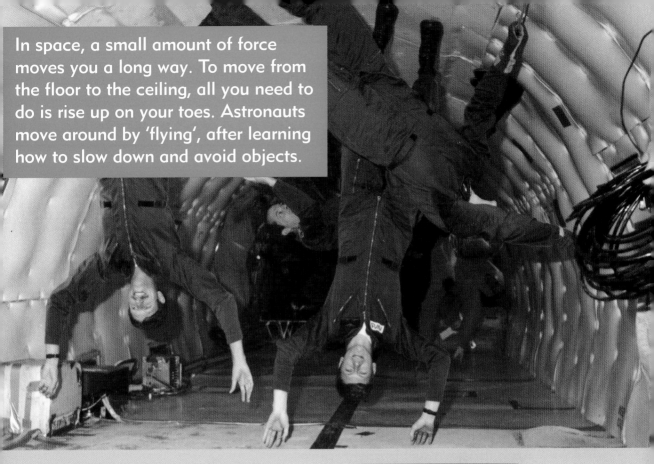

Exercise also helps combat 'puffy face syndrome' where blood rushes to the head and upper body because there is little gravity.

GO FACT!
DID YOU KNOW?
Handholds are mounted inside and outside the ISS to help astronauts maintain their direction.

Preparation for a Spacewalk

Spacesuits have lower pressure than the space station, so an astronaut must take certain steps to avoid getting **decompression sickness**, known as 'the bends'.

Before a spacewalk an astronaut needs to breathe pure oxygen for two hours and 20 minutes. This helps to removes excess nitrogen from the bloodstream. An astronaut will breathe pure oxygen during all the following steps.

What you need:

- pressurised spacesuit (after 25 spacewalks, return the suit to Earth for maintenance)
- oxygen mask
- cycle ergometer (exercise bike)

What to do:

1 Move into the Joint Airlock Module and cycle on the ergometer for 10 minutes.

2 Put on a pressurised spacesuit, trousers first.

3 Put on the pressurised spacesuit jacket.

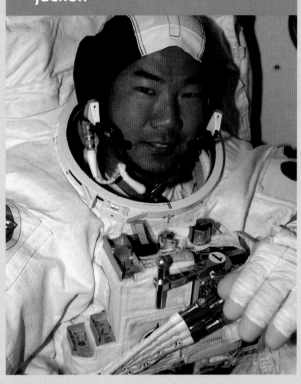

4 Move towards the airlock door.

5 Move out into space and begin the spacewalk.

Probes

Space probes are sent into space by rockets. Probes are robots that carry scientific instruments. They either orbit, land on, or fly by planets, sending pictures and data back to Earth.

New Horizons

Probes have visited every classical planet in the solar system. A probe called New Horizons was launched in January 2006. It will fly by dwarf planet Pluto in 2015. The plan is for the probe to also explore the **Kuiper Belt**.

Scientists hope to learn more about Saturn's rings and moons from the Cassini/Huygens mission. It began transmitting information in 2004. The Huygens probe landed on Titan, one of Saturn's moons, in January 2005.

Two probes, Pioneer 10 and Pioneer 11, were launched in 1973 and are heading for outer space. Pioneer 10 has already sent back images of Jupiter and is now heading for the star Aldebaran. This trip will take two million years. Attached to Pioneer 10 is a metal **plaque** giving information about how to find Earth.

The Voyager probes are also heading into outer space. Voyager 1 is 10.8 billion kilometres (6.7 billion miles) from Earth and is headed towards a **dwarf star**, which it should reach in 400 000 years. Voyager 2 is headed towards the star, Sirius. This journey will take over 350 000 years.

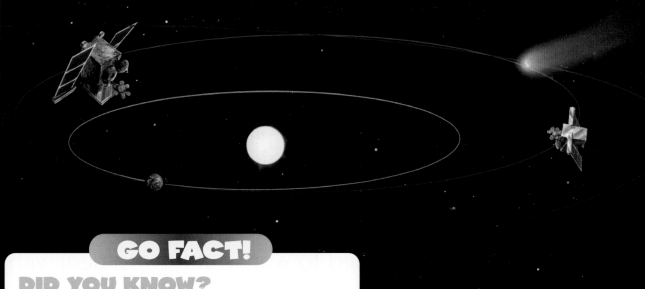

DID YOU KNOW?

Probes also explore **asteroids** and **comets**. In 2004 the Stardust probe flew through the cloud of dust and gas around the comet Wild 2, collecting particles and taking photographs. It brought the contents back to Earth in a return capsule.

Probes often use one planet's gravity like a slingshot. The probe gets a boost in speed so it can continue further into space.

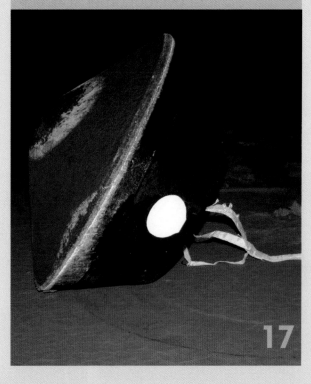

The Stardust probe safely arrived back on Earth in January 2006.

Landing on Mars

Probes have visited Mars, but no humans have walked on the red planet. Before humans can visit Mars, we need to work out how to deal with the hostile environment.

2001 Mars Odyssey

Mars is cold, and as far as we know, dry. The 2001 Mars Odyssey probe was sent to Mars in 2001 to search for water. The probe is orbiting the planet and using **gamma rays** to look underground. If water is discovered, other spacecraft can drill for water in preparation for human explorers.

In January 2004, two robotic 'rovers', called Spirit and Opportunity, landed on Mars. They explored the surface of Mars, looking for evidence of water. The rovers communicate directly with Earth via Odyssey.

Odyssey also contains an instrument to measure radiation levels, both on the trip to Mars, and on the planet itself. Once these levels are established, scientists will be able to determine the possible effects on astronauts. Engineers can then design equipment to protect people from the effects of radiation.

Mars projects on Earth

To develop techniques for living in harsh environments, people will live in the rocky, polar regions in the Arctic. Though nothing like Mars, these regions are the closest conditions on Earth to those on Mars. This will help provide new technologies for the future exploration of Mars.

Astronauts on Mars may be able to use elements such as methane and oxygen in the Martian atmosphere to make fuel for their return journey.

It could take up to nine months for a spacecraft to reach Mars, deploy a lander craft and actually land on the surface of Mars.

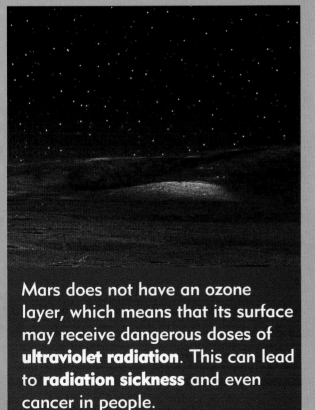

Mars does not have an ozone layer, which means that its surface may receive dangerous doses of **ultraviolet radiation**. This can lead to **radiation sickness** and even cancer in people.

GO FACT!

DID YOU KNOW?

Scientists are working on rockets with plasma engines that could reduce the flight to Mars to about three months. This would reduce the length of time that astronauts are exposed to radiation and microgravity.

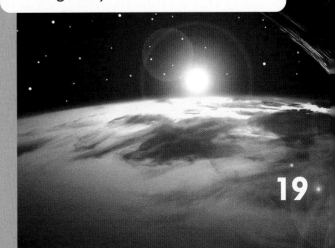

# Base on the Moon

Although people have already walked on the Moon, there are plans for further exploration, and even a permanent settlement on the Moon.

Some people believe that the Moon is a ready-made space station. Further exploration of space could occur from a Moon base. As there is less gravity, spacecraft would need less energy to take off from the Moon than they do from Earth.

Water ice has been discovered at the Moon's **poles**. This could be melted for drinking water, and broken down into oxygen for breathing and hydrogen for rocket fuel. Water would not need to be transported from Earth. Once enclosed areas were built, people could grow plants.

The south pole of the Moon is an ideal position for a base. This site can provide water ice. There is also a mountain which receives almost continuous sunlight. If solar panels were installed, a Moon base could use solar energy.

Opponents of a permanent Moon base believe enough money has already been spent on exploring the Moon. If we plan to send further expeditions to the Moon it will take resources away from Mars exploration.

There is also argument about whether the ice discovered on the Moon can be easily extracted and used for water.

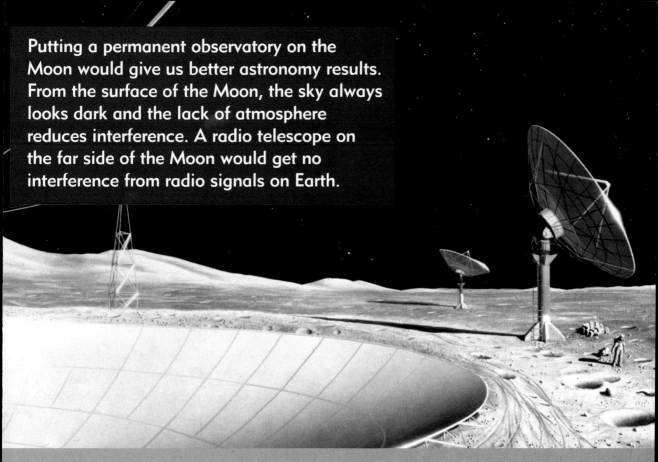

Putting a permanent observatory on the Moon would give us better astronomy results. From the surface of the Moon, the sky always looks dark and the lack of atmosphere reduces interference. A radio telescope on the far side of the Moon would get no interference from radio signals on Earth.

There are plans to mine the helium-3 that exists on the Moon. Scientists are still learning how to use helium-3 for energy production. It is hoped that it will be an efficient and clean fuel source.

GO FACT!

DID YOU KNOW?
It would take one Earth year to make a return trip to Mars from the Moon.

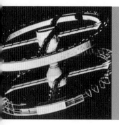

Space Settlements

Space settlements are enclosed areas in orbit. Scientists believe that people will live in these settlements sometime in the future.

Space settlements could be in the shape of a sphere, cylinder, or even a doughnut, but they must be airtight, so they maintain air pressure and a breathable atmosphere. They must also rotate in order to create artificial gravity. This means that people won't have to cope with the effects of microgravity, such as muscle wasting and loss of bone density.

Space settlements need constant sunlight to produce solar power. They also need some sort of barrier to protect them from the Sun's radiation. On Earth, our atmosphere provides this protection. Later settlements may decide to leave our solar system, but they will still need protection from the radiation of other stars.

People living in space may still want regular contact and visits to Earth. Therefore, spacecraft launches from both Earth and the settlement will need to be cheap. An environmentally-safe method of launching craft from Earth needs to be invented, due to the risk to the Earth's atmosphere from a large number of launches.

Space settlements in orbit would lack materials, such as metals. These would have to be imported from the Moon, or from nearby asteroids. Transporting such materials from Earth would be too expensive.

It is planned that each settlement will be self-contained, so everything that is produced will need to be recycled, such as water, oxygen and waste.

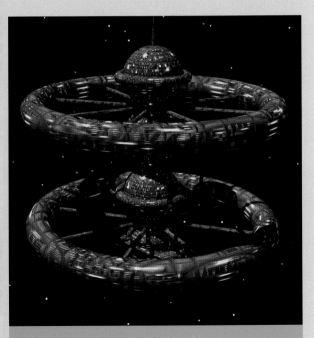

No liveable space settlements have been built yet, but many have been imagined by science fiction writers and movie producers.

GO FACT!

DID YOU KNOW?

NASA has studied the possibility of building space settlements in orbit. They believe it is possible, as plenty of the necessary materials are available on the Moon or on asteroids. The Sun could supply the necessary energy. NASA believes no new scientific breakthroughs are necessary, but lots of engineering would be required.

Sails, Slingshots and More

NASA is working on more efficient methods of taking us into space in the future.

How about going via **antimatter** spacecraft? The idea is to build engines that combine matter and antimatter. The resulting explosion would give enormous **thrust** to a spacecraft. It would take one month to reach Mars.

Magnetic levitation spacecraft are like catapults. The spacecraft hovers on a magnetic field above a track that heads into space. When the spacecraft reaches the end of the track, rockets would take over and sling it into space.

Travel to the ISS could be by one of a variety of space vehicles NASA is working on. They are designing spacecraft that will work alongside the space shuttles. The spacecraft are small vehicles that will carry three to six crew members and small amounts of cargo.

One proposed method of taking robotic equipment further into space is solar sails. A huge sail, made from carbon fibres, **unfurls** in space. The sail is then propelled by reflecting sunlight. It will start very slowly but, after absorbing energy from the Sun, it could move up to five times faster than current rockets.

Electronic catapults on the Moon could launch bulk materials to settlements in orbit.

The Crew Return Vehicle could be used as an emergency vehicle between the International Space Station and Earth.

Other types of spacecraft could be inflated in space – NASA scientists are working on inflatable telescopes and antennae.

25

Space Tourism

There are plans for tourist space travel and an orbiting space hotel.

In May 2001, the first paying space tourist visited the International Space Station. Dennis Tito paid the Russian Space Agency $20 million (£10.6 million) for eight days on the station.

Some private corporations are developing plans to construct hotels in space. One corporation, Space Island Group, proposed building its rotating hotel from the space shuttles' external fuel tanks, after they have been **jettisoned**. Another corporation is planning to build a cruise ship that will fly between Earth's orbit and the Moon.

NASA is also looking at inflatable **habitats** for space. One idea is to attach a three-storey inflatable to the ISS. Of course, it is looking carefully at the strength of the materials. The inflatable has to be strong enough to resist **space debris**.

A sealed habitat like this could also be used as a Moon base or living quarters on Mars. At the moment NASA intends these for the use of scientists only, but at a later stage similar habitats could be used for tourists.

Some of the largest and wealthiest companies on Earth, such as British Airways, Hilton and Virgin have shown great interest in constructing space hotels.

The company Bigelow Aerospace is planning to officially launch the first space hotel, named Nautilus, by 2010.

Orbiting space hotels might be reached by Horus space planes. These planes would be launched from a rocket.

Space Technologies

Space programs develop technologies which will benefit people on Earth.

Solar power could be improved, by beaming the Sun's rays down to Earth using solar panels in orbit. The solar energy will be converted into laser or microwave beams and sent to Earth to provide power.

Purer **protein crystals** can be grown in space than on Earth. By studying these crystals, scientists will better understand the nature of proteins and viruses, perhaps leading to the development of new drugs. This type of research could lead to possible treatments for cancer and other diseases.

Some experiments will study the space environment itself and how long-term exposure to space, the vacuum and debris affects materials. This research will provide future spacecraft designers and scientists with a better understanding of space, and it will improve spacecraft design.

Some experiments will study the basic forces of nature. These experiments take advantage of the weightlessness of space to study forces that are difficult to study on Earth because of its gravity. This research could lead to clocks a thousand times more accurate than today's **atomic clocks**, better weather forecasting and stronger materials.

Other planets, asteroids and even comets may be a source of fuels/minerals in the future.

Living cells can be grown in space where they are not distorted by gravity. These cells can be used to test new treatments for cancer, with less risk to patients.

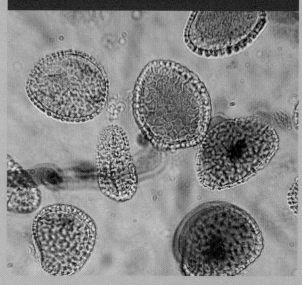

Experiments with a device that can create gravity ranging from almost zero to twice that of Earth, will be carried out on the ISS. This facility will **simulate** the gravity on the Moon or Mars, for experiments that can provide information useful for future space travels.

GO FACT!

DID YOU KNOW?

The results of future research in space will benefit people on Earth not only by providing new products as a result, but also by creating new jobs to make the products.

Table

Many people question why we spend so much money on going to space. They argue that the money could be better spent on getting rid of poverty down here on Earth. What many people don't realise is that mankind benefits greatly from space exploration. This table provides a small sample of some of the benefits.

What?	Benefits
Weather forecasting	Technology used in the space shuttle program is now being applied to weather forecasting. This technology continually monitors the atmosphere and is much more accurate than older forecasting technology.
Cancer detection	Image sensor chips used in the Hubble Space Telescope are being used in medical **digital imaging**. The digital images can be used instead of **biopsies**, which cause pain and scarring.
Cool suit	Spacesuits have provided the inspiration for a 'cool suit' which circulates **coolant** around a person and lowers their body temperature. This can benefit people who have multiple sclerosis, cerebral palsy and spina bifida.
Community safety	Many projects undertaken by NASA have resulted in improvements to safety in the community. Examples are a lightweight fireman's tank, personal alarm systems, emergency rescue cutters and a self-righting life raft. Robots are now used for hazardous tasks that would otherwise be done by humans.
Tissue stimulator	This device is implanted in the body to help patients control chronic pain by stimulating certain nerves, or specific areas of the brain, with electricity.
Water purification	NASA developed water purification systems for developing nations. They use iodine instead of chlorine.
Skin damage assessment	In burns cases, **ultrasound** technology developed by NASA is used to assess the depth of the burns. This helps when making a decision about the best type of treatment.
Other benefits	Other benefits from the space program include fire-resistant materials, better brakes, aircraft engines, ribbed swimsuits, more accurate golf balls, athletic shoes and improved school bus design.

# Glossary

airlock module an airtight chamber, located between two areas of unequal pressure, in which air pressure is controlled

antimatter matter consisting of particles that are the opposite of those making up normal matter

asteroids hundreds of minor planets that lie mainly between Mars and Jupiter

atomic clock the most accurate type of clock in the world, designed to measure time according to vibrations within atoms

biopsy the removal of a small part of a person's body to check if it is diseased

comet a body in space that moves around the Sun; consists of a bright central part which is surrounded by a misty part that finishes in a tail

coolant a liquid or gas used to reduce the temperature of something

cosmonaut a person trained to take part in the flight of a spacecraft

decompression sickness a dangerous condition where nitrogen bubbles form in the blood and other tissues of the body; caused by a rapid decrease in the pressure surrounding the body

dehydrate lose water or other fluids

density closely packed together

digital imaging computer scanned images which may be subsequently edited, displayed or printed

dock to close and lock one spacecraft into another spacecraft, while in orbit

dwarf star a smaller-sized star (our Sun is a yellow dwarf star)

gamma rays high-energy waves that come from a radioactive source

habitat a dwelling

heat-stabilise heat-process and store in can

interplanetary situated between planets

jettison throw cargo overboard to lighten the weight of a vessel

Kuiper Belt region of minor planets and ice outside the orbit of Neptune

magnetic levitation the process by which an object is suspended above another object with no other support than magnetic fields

microgravity very weak gravity

plaque a metal plate with information on it

poles opposite ends of a planet

protein crystals clear, transparent substances that are important for life; resembling ice

radiation sickness physical illness caused by exposure to large doses of radiation

solar array series of connected solar cells; a panel that collects power from the Sun

solar cells devices that convert sunlight directly to electricity

Soviet Union a large group of countries in eastern Europe and northern Asia, mainly made up of Russia. This group split up in 1991 and no longer exists.

space debris pieces of rockets, satellites and other objects left in space by man's activities

simulate imitate; reproduce

thrust force produced by an engine that drives an aircraft forward

ultrasound the use of sound waves to see inside the body

ultraviolet radiation invisible rays in sunlight that cause suntan, sunburn, premature skin aging and most cases of skin cancer

unfurls unfolds or unrolls

water ice water frozen in the solid state

Index